To:

May you find peace, hope,
and beauty in all of
your silver linings.

From:

silver linings

marie d. jones

new seasons™

a division of Publications International, Ltd.

Louis Weber, CEO
Publications International, Ltd.
7373 North Cicero Avenue
Lincolnwood, Illinois 60712

Manufactured in China.

ISBN 0-7853-4370-9

Original inspirations by Marie D. Jones

Compiled inspirations by Joan Loshek

Marie D. Jones is a licensed New Thought minister and is also in practitioner
training for ministerial status in Religious Science. She is widely published in
both books and magazines and has contributed to titles including *Bless This
Marriage*, *The Ruby Book of Love*, and *The Sapphire Book of Inspiration*.

Acknowledgments:
Publications International, Ltd., has made every effort to locate the owners of
all copyrighted material to obtain permission to use the selections that appear
in this book. Any errors or omissions are unintentional; corrections, if
necessary, will be made in future editions.

Scripture quotations taken from the *New Revised Standard Version of the
Bible*, copyright © 1989, by the Division of Christian Education of the
National Council of the Churches of Christ in the United States of America.
Used by permission. All rights reserved.

contents

Love's Promise

As I gaze upon the faces of my
family and friends,
I thank my lucky stars above for
love that never ends.
No matter where I travel or
how far away I roam,
The greatest blessings God can give
are found right here at home.

*L*ove is often
most fully expressed
by the smallest of gestures:
a kind smile, a helping hand,
a comfortable shoulder.

silver linings

love's promise

silver linings

love's promise

Where there is love,
there is light.
Where there is light,
there is wisdom.
Where there is wisdom,
there is understanding.
Where there is understanding,
there is love.

love's promise

*N*obody has
ever measured,
even poets,
how much a
heart can hold.

Zelda Fitzgerald (1900–1948)

silver linings

love's promise

silver linings

love's promise

In the garden of my life,
one difference I have found—
most flowers only bloom in spring,
but love blooms all year round.

Love comforteth like sunshine
after rain.

William Shakespeare

silver linings

love's promise

silver linings

love's promise

Love is the healer of broken
hearts that long to be made whole.
Love is the lighthouse beacon that
brings lost souls safely back to shore.
Love is the guide that directs
each footstep through the forest of
hopes and dreams. Love is the
answer to every question, the
fulfillment of every need.

Life's Journey

*P*ast memories,
present experiences,
future dreams—
all are but different spokes
upon the wheel of life.
Each turn of the wheel
reminds us of where we came from,
of who we are today,
and of what we hope to become.

life's journey

*T*o laugh often and much;
To win the respect of intelligent people
and the affection of children;
To earn the appreciation of honest

silver linings

critics and endure the
betrayal of false friends;
To appreciate beauty;
To find the best in others;
To leave the world a bit better,
whether by a healthy child, a garden
patch or a redeemed social condition;
To know even one life has breathed
easier because you have lived;
That is to have succeeded.

Ralph Waldo Emerson

life's journey

Upon the journey of your life,
the road will
sometimes split in two.
One path is the old.
The other, new.
Which one you choose
is up to you.

silver linings

life's journey

Each life is like a
patchwork quilt created from
the fabric of experience,
the texture of character,
and the color of personality,
all lovingly handmade
by a divine designer.

With maturity comes the
courage and ability to
slow the hectic pace of life.
The wise know that a journey is
meaningless without occasionally
stopping to enjoy the view.

silver linings

life's journey

silver linings

life's journey

Let the experiences of the past be like the powerful wake that propels your boat forward into the vast and limitless ocean of new discovery. Let wisdom be the sails that guide you, and let your heart's desire be the wind that moves you over the sea.

For everything there is a
season, and a time for every
matter under heaven:
a time to be born,
and a time to die;
a time to plant,
and a time to pluck up
what is planted.

Ecclesiastes 3:1–2

silver linings

life's journey

silver linings

life's journey

*L*ook to each sunset not as the ending of a day, but as a time of rest and renewal before another day dawns. So it is with life—with each ending comes a new beginning, an eternal circle of dawns and sunsets.

Bright Horizons

silver linings

Is there a desire you would
like to pursue
but feel it's too late to start?
Is there a goal that you long to fulfill
or a dream that still tugs
at your heart?
Then today is the day
to move forward in faith
and to follow the callings within.
For no matter your age
or the time that has passed,
it's never too late to begin.

bright horizons

silver linings

bright horizons

What is the
measure of a life well lived?
What is the meaning of success?
To travel through life
with those we love
is the ticket to happiness.

Pleasures
newly found are sweet
When they lie about our feet.

William Wordsworth (1770–1850)

silver linings

bright horizons

silver linings

bright horizons

There are places I have been
where memories abound,
of folks I met along the way
and happiness I found.
Now I set my sights upon
new visions to fulfill,
and know that what I find there
will be even grander still.

Think of all
the beauty still
left around you
and be happy.

Anne Frank, **Diary of a Young Girl** *(1952)*

silver linings

bright horizons

silver linings

bright horizons

No matter our
age or where we've been
or what we've said and done,
each sunrise is a reminder that
we've only just begun.

Bountiful Blessings

$\mathcal{L}$ife is a cornucopia overflowing
with a harvest of bountiful blessings.
Love, family, health, and happiness
are the ripe and abundant fruits
of a life well lived.

silver linings

bountiful blessings

still find each day too
short for all the thoughts I want to
think, all the walks I want to take,
all the books I want to read,
and all the friends I want to see.

John Burroughs (1837–1921)

*A*wake each morning
in gratitude for the blessing of
another day, for each is a precious
gift and a priceless opportunity
to live, to laugh, and to love.

silver linings

bountiful blessings

silver linings

bountiful blessings

silver linings

I peeked inside a rosebud
and was surprised to see
the face of the creator
smiling back at me.

I gazed upon a daisy
and surely I could tell
that who or what created it
loved it very well.

bountiful blessings

I am beginning
to learn that it is the sweet,
simple things of life which are the
real ones after all.

Laura Ingalls Wilder (1867–1957)

silver linings

bountiful blessings

silver linings

bountiful blessings

*M*iracles are not only ecstatic visions or holy interventions visited upon the chosen few. Every moment we are alive is full of reasons to sing out in joyful gratitude. Every breath we are given is a reminder that the glory of life is at hand. In the people we love, in the beauty of nature, in the golden sun that rises each morning—miracles are everywhere.

bountiful blessings

Try to count the blades of grass
upon a gentle slope
or the grains of sand along a
stretch of beach or the shining
stars in the vast night sky.
To do this is to come face-to-face
with the universe's beauty
and abundance.

silver linings

bountiful blessings

Serenity's Path

I walk serenity's path
to a place of inner peace and quiet
solitude. Here in the stillness,
I hear the voice of wisdom.
Here in the stillness,
I feel my spirit soar.

serenity's path

*B*efore me peaceful,
Behind me peaceful,
Under me peaceful,
Over me peaceful,
All around me peaceful.

Navajo saying

silver linings

serenity's path

silver linings

serenity's path

There is poetry in nature,
sweet music on the breeze,
each flower's a sonata played
in tune with honeybees.

In quiet contemplation,
I can hear the song take flight,
sung in perfect harmony,
so lyrical and light.

In the midst
of each busy, noisy day,
there is a calm and peaceful place
at the center of your being
where you can go
to replenish your weary spirit.

silver linings

serenity's path

silver linings

serenity's path

To walk in balance,
we first must center ourselves
in the present moment,
with no regrets of the past
and no worries for the future.
With our hearts at peace and
our minds calm, we can walk
in grace and beauty.

*W*orking in the garden...gives me a profound feeling of inner peace. Nothing here is in a hurry. There is no rush toward accomplishment, no blowing of trumpets. Here is the great mystery of life and growth. Everything is changing, growing, aiming at something, but silently, unboastfully, taking its time.

Ruth Stout

silver linings

serenity's path

silver linings

serenity's path

The outer world
is like a mirror
reflecting back
whatever you give
from within.
Give love, and the world
loves you back.
Give peace, and the world
becomes more peaceful.
Give light, and the world
will be a little brighter.